Fatherless Child

You Are Never Alone

Spoken Words by

Abraham Ali

This book is dedicated to
Jasmine, Daniel, and Elijah,
the children who set me free
and taught me how to be
me. To a young man named
Tony. In countless boys and
girls who are incarcerated in
juvenile prisons across this
country. I fight, and I write,
on your behalf.

I love you more than you
hate yourself.
— Master Fard Muhammad

I am committed to breaking
the cycle of self-destruction.
One soul at a time.

Poems From the Soul

Crack Was My Religion. . . . 3

Ten Minutes of Trauma . . . 7

Sisters Who Raised Me. . . 13

Erase the Pain 16

Trapped in the triple
    darkness of my mind . . 20

The Caged Bird. 23

The Night the Cold Stole
    My Soul. 27

Can you hear the tears?. . 30

Will you cry for me? 37

L.D. ME 40

You are Moor 43

I Write 46

Speak It Into Existence . . 50

Woman 56

I'm Sorry 58

No One Listens 61

Let's Meditate 66

I Am Alive 72

I cannot imagine how you
   must feel 80

A Mother's Pain 85

Tears of Bondage 89

Remember Me 95

War 102

It's Okay to Cry 104

I Forgive Me 107

My Declaration 111

I'm Tired of Thinking . . . 113

Will you help me heal? . . 118

Poetry 123

Secret Weapon 126

Silence Speaks 132

Slipping Into Darkness . . 135

I was not born to judge you,
    I was born to love you 140

I AM 145

Today I Made a Decision 147

Bob Marley 152

Be a Father 156

G.O.A.L.S. (God Over All
    Life's Successes) 161

Light 164

Me 167

Know Thy Self 168

Love Yourself 169

Black Fire 171

Mystic Memories 174

Father Farrakhan (Special
  Thanks) 177

I am Abraham Ali 181

Fatherless Child

You Are Never Alone

FRONT LINE
REDSKINS

Ye are all gods
Children of the
Most High God
— Psalm 82:6

Don't expect anything
but know that you're
worthy of everything

Crack Was My Religion

At the age of 12, I made a
decision
To make crack cocaine the
god of my religion
I was baptized in the hellfire
of cocaine smoke
Anointed with the power to
deceive
Possessed by the spirit of
pain
As I sold my soul in vain to
the drug game
Blind, death, and dumb
I fell in love with the nigger
I became

Welcome to my house of
shame

O, what a faithful servant I
became
As he began to mold me in
his image and likeness
Shaping me in my own
iniquities
Preparing me for my destiny
As I slowly digested his
recipe
In total submission, I gave
him the best of me
Captivated by the illusion in
which once was confusion
Now became clear, the
reason why I am here

Chosen with passion and
    purpose
I could now execute his
    service
Standing confident and bold
I began to kill souls

The older I grew
The colder I grew
And the innocent little boy
That I once knew
I no longer knew
I could not recognize his
    face
For he had entered into a
    place
A state of disgrace
A state of unconsciousness
Where I was alive but not

awake
For I had chosen my faith
And accepted my fate.

Ten Minutes
of Trauma

The me that you can't see
Trapped inside the trauma
    that this world creates
Born to dictate my fate
But will I ever escape the
    pain of self-hate
Six hundred seconds of
    anxiety
Confined, every time I look
    inside a book
It reminds me of my
    disability
Unable to perceive
Mocked and teased
Because I can't read

Physically abused by my
    teacher
Miseducated by my preacher
How long will this torture
    last
Labeled L.D.
Suffering in the mind of
    dyslexic me
I hate you to a degree

Ten minutes of trauma feels
    like a lifetime to me
Words cannot describe what
    I see
Confused, abused, and left
    alone to suffer in silence
The only way I can express
    myself was through anger
    and violence

I was a victim and the world
was to blame
Welcome to my 10 minutes
of shame
Six hundred seconds of
eternal pain
Trapped inside the trauma of
a dyslexic brain
Every second, I am dwelling
in a mental prison of
depression
So hard to breathe
I just wanna leave
Tell me, is there a cure for
this disease

Ten minutes of trauma feels
like a lifetime to me
Six hundred seconds, the

clock is ticking
It's your turn to read out
  loud
I am crying from the inside
  out
But nothing comes out
I tried my best but I could
  never pass the test
Ten minutes of trauma that
  will never rest
Six hundred seconds of
  anxiety at its best
This is the countdown to my
  final breath
Feels like a lifetime to my
  dyslexic mind

I can't learn what you see
There's no teacher who

could teach me
From elementary to high
    school
I was convinced I was a fool
Deaf, dumb, and blind
The enslavement of the
    mind
The pipeline to prison
This is the trauma that
    shaped and molded my
    every decision
Six hundred seconds feels
    like a lifetime to me
Ten minutes of trauma, I am
    blind but I still see
Can someone teach me to
    read and write
I cannot even spell my name
Ten years old, dwelling in

shame
Ten minutes of torture and
  pain
How long will this trauma
  remain
Welcome to my dyslexic
  brain
Ten minutes of trauma feels
  like a lifetime to me
10, 9, 8, 7, 6, 5, 4, 3, 2, 1
I am numb
I do not feel what you feel
Please believe me, you
  would not want to be
  dyslexic me
Six hundred seconds feels
  like a lifetime to me.

Sisters Who Raised Me

In honor of the sisters who
raised me
The unconditional love and
wisdom that made me
Mesmerized by the smile of
your twin
When I see you, I see the
beauty within

The oneness of the mother
and daughter's love
The passion and commitment
are a gift from the
heavens above
Such a joy to be in your
presence

I am forever grateful for
   your divine essence
Your willing to sacrifice your
   life
So that your children can
   experience eternal life

Congratulations to my
   sisters of the Sun
We have a new life,
   enjoyment has begun
A new baby to raise, to love
   and teach
An extension of our family
Another soul for your
   beauty to reach

Orion, Jasmine, and Elijah
Through them you will live

forever
They are the gift, the
    treasure
That no amount of wealth
    can measure
You taught me and my
    brother to discover
The love within, the greatest
    friend

This is dedicated to the
    twins, mercy and grace
A mother's love, a
    grandmother's love cannot
    be replaced
Wisdom is the only
    foundation upon their face
Every day they grow in
    beauty.

Erase the Pain

Now I embrace the pain
I erase the past
Leaving no trace of darkness

Now I emerge into the light
Defining my future, it is so
    bright
For eyes cannot see my
    destiny
I can only imagine who I'm
    destined to be

Blessed with God's recipe
To deliver me unto Eternity
360 degrees
I am infinity

Truly humbled to receive my
    identity
Forever grateful, forever
    thankful
To be surrounded by mercy
    and grace
I stand firm on my square
Meditating in my outer space
Right now, I am in that Holy
    place face-to-face

As I embrace His loving faith
I bear witness to this divine
    mind state
Blessed with the ability to
    recreate
And fashion into shape
With the power to dictate
    my own fate

We were born to create
Accept your nature now
Please don't wait
Tomorrow might be too late.

They say it's easier
said than done
I say it's easier done
than said

Trapped in the triple darkness of my mind

I seek strength and might
   in the darkness of my
   weakness
I will continue to fight with
   passion and power until
   my final hour
Time will not define me and
   the past will not remind
   me of my pain
I will no longer be confined
   by my shame
I will not remain the victim
   of my decisions
Trapped in this lonely prison

I can no longer blame
    another name
I am responsible for how
    long this pain remains
How strong are these chains
That shackle my shame
Dwelling in a prison of pride
Living on the edge of suicide
    and homicide

Don't push me off the bridge
I might kill you
No, I don't hear you
Screaming for your life
I am deaf to the eternal
    breath
I am numb to what I have
    done
Dumb is the total sum

I am blind to my crime
So in the shadows of my
  actions
I am confined
Trapped in the triple
  darkness of my mind.

The Caged Bird

I know why the caged bird
 sings
She's crying to be redeemed
She is lost in-between
 reality and a dream
She'll be free but she'll still
 be slave
Raised in a cage of
 deception
She sings the melody of the
 resurrection
This bird is destined to fly
 high
She refuses to be silent

She has been a victim of

violets separated then
   violated
Her innocence has been
   shattered, penetrated by
   self-hate
Now she carries the weight
   of death
She feels haunted by her
   every breath
Her voice was the only thing
   that she had left
Her will to speak quietly fell
   asleep
She chose to stay in that
   sacred place
Until it was time for the
   world to hear her passion
   and grace

She is the hope for the
    hopeless and the voice for
    the voiceless
She chose to sing for the
    choiceless
This caged bird has been set
    free
And the whole planet is her
    destiny
Please continue to fly and
    sing
So we can see an example
    of how it looks to be
    redeemed
We will follow the vibration
    of your voice

This caged bird sings
    because she made the

right choice
She decided to listen to her
   internal voice
And share her story as she
   sings the melody of true
   Glory
Every cage bird has a story
So join the chorus to be free
And sing with me
For freedom, justice, and
   equality is our destiny.

The Night the Cold Stole My Soul

One cold, late December
  night
That I will remember for the
  rest of my life
Heartbeat racing 100 miles
  an hour
As I reach the peak of
  passion and power
In bracing the weakness of
  my pain
Now trapped in the darkness
  of my shame
As I flee the scene
I can hear the screams of
  death

A soul taking its final breath
The cry echoes like the
  sound of a wild animal
Being slaughtered in the
  wilderness

The further I ran with his
  blood stained upon my
  hands
Lost in a maze, I thought
I could take this darkness to
  my grave
The second life sentence I
  escaped
Mercy and grace must have
  a purpose for my fate
But wait, I can't masturbate
  with justice
Because she will come

She is like the setting in the
rising of the sun
The judgment day has
begun.

Can you hear
the tears?

Can you hear the little boy
Crying inside the man that
 I am
Because I can hear the
 little girl crying inside my
 mother
I can hear my grandmother's
 tears
I can feel the pain of the
 little boy inside my
 brother
As I reflect on my father's
 fears
Drowning in the tears of
 depression

In the darkness of my
    anxiety
Screaming to be free in the
    silence of my misery
Who hears me
When my father speaks
I can hear the voice of a
    wounded child crying
    out loud
For someone to relieve the
    suffering little boy within
Can you hear him
Can you hear them
Screaming to be redeemed
The voices of God's children
The tears of history
The deepest ocean of
    emotion
We are all learning how to

swim in
Tears of fear
Tears of pain
Tears of joy
These are the tears of the
   little boy
That lives within crying
In the darkness of my mind
Where my memories become
   a crime
Shackled in shame
The tears of a victim
Where everyone else is the
   blame for my pain
I can hear the little me
   crying inside
Paralyzed by pride and
   shame
Can you hear the tears of

the fatherless child
She suffers in silence
Fear is her best friend
Self-hate is their sin
The little boy that lives
    within men
The little girl that can't
    comprehend
The absence of him
They feel so alone
The father that never came
    home to his throne
Your children just want you
    to come back home
We miss you.

Your pain is a reflection
of your power

Seek guidance within
because you are
not without

Will you cry
for me?

Will you cry for the little
boy who cried himself
to sleep

Will you cry for the little
boy who never deserved
to be beat

Will you cry for the little
boy who endured pain
and self-hate

Will you cry for the little
boy who would one day
allow anger to dictate
his fate

Will you cry for the little
   boy who carried the
   burden of sin

Will you cry for the little
   boy who would not allow
   love to enter in

Will you cry for the little
   boy abused and left alone

Will you cry for the little
   boy lost, trying to find his
   way home

Will you cry for the little
   boy who suffered in
   silence

Will you cry for the little
   boy who would one day
   express his pain through
   violence

Will you cry for the little
   boy who believed in his
   preacher

Will you cry for the little
   boy who was brutally
   beaten by his teacher

Will you cry for the little
   boy

Will you cry for me?

L.D. ME

I write on behalf of the
    illiterate

Consider it a blessing
If you can read and write
Millions were not gifted with
    that insight

I write to inspire the
    dyslexic mind
Those who feel they are
    deaf, dumb, and blind
Mentally confined
Can't see pass their ADHD
Chained to anxiety

I write on behalf of the
    learning disabled
Agitated and confused
Frustrated and depressed
Convinced that none of this
    makes sense

I write to reach those that
    the teachers can't teach
They cannot reach the minds
    that are confined
In the darkness of their
    shame because
They can't even spell or
    read their own name

I write to inspire them
To light the natural fire
    within

I write to restore their
  memory
To insure their legacy
I write because I am their
  destiny
And we are destined to be
  free.

You are Moor

You are more, so much more
You are not your thoughts
You are not your experience,
 don't be convinced
There is not enough
 evidence to prove that
 is you

You are more
More than your pain
More than your name
The titles, the labels, the
 idols
You are more than your past
You are more than your
 present state, your future
 is great

You are so much more than
   your self-hate

Your destination is bright
You are more, you are the
   light
You are more than the
   image that we see on TV,
   Facebook, and Instagram
You are more than your
   fame
All the money, diamonds,
   cars, and ice
Could never compare to the
   value of your life

You are more
Your treasure we cannot
   measure

44

You are more valuable than
all that we have and will
ever receive
You are so much more
Don't just believe
You must know.

I Write

I write for the rejected
  stone
The young child who got
  lost trying to find his way
  home
Drowning in the pain of his
  decisions
Enslaved in this mental state
  of prison
I write for those in captivity,
  in bondage
Dwelling in a state of triple
  darkness
I write for the mentally
  insane
Who cannot articulate and

express their internal pain
Most of them die in vain
Or suffer in silence while
    caged at war with their
    own inner violence

We are the voice for the
    voiceless
And the hope for the
    hopeless
We choose for the
    choiceless to be free
I write for more than just
    me
Freedom, justice, and
    equality
For all, I write as a witness
    of the final call

I write to paint a new picture
I write on behalf of those
    who have passed on
Have transitioned into the
    light and experienced
The ultimate sacrifice of life
Their energy has survived
    and we are committed
To make sure they stay alive

I write on behalf of Mother
    Earth
God's divine universal nurse
She has endured this curse
She has given birth to the
    worse and the best
She is beyond blessed

I write to give sight to the

blind
Speak it into existence
ART4LYFE. Frontline State of
Mind.

Speak It Into Existence

Write it into existence
We write from an infinite
    place, a divine space in
    time
Out of the triple darkness
    of our mind
We emerge with words
Traveling at the speed of
    light
Wisdom possessed with the
    power to penetrate
Dictate and fashion into
    shape
Vibrating at a rate that is
    destined to create

Harnessing the energy of
the Universe
Through our revelation, we
elevate
Through our words, we
levitate
As we speak our truth into
existence
We demonstrate the force
and power of the spoken
word to procreate
Something out of nothing
In the absence of our
thoughts, we meditate

In the silence of our
imagination
We become one with the
Author of Creation

This is the process of divine
    revelation
As we breathe these words
    into existence
With no resistance, in
    complete submission

On our mission, we rely on
    our sacred intuition
Guided and protected by
    our chi
We released the ego and
    embrace our identity
Pure electricity
Writing from a place of no
    mind
The absence of time
The state of now
The presence of perfection

Illuminated light, we write
   for a purpose
To produce sight in the
   darkest night
So we will write it into
   existence
Until it is our reality
So continue to write
Continue to recite.

FRONT LINE

There is a way out of
the darkness
It is within the light

Woman

It is my honor, my mission,
  my duty
To protect and serve
To respect and preserve
Everything that they
  represent is heaven sent

I am convinced that they
  are the evidence that God
  exists
Every day I thank the Father
  for their presence
And the ability to endure
  the pain
Embrace the shame and
  never live a day in vain

Thank you for this present,
    the gift of our essence
They gave me life, they
    raised me right
Guided me through the
    darkest night
In hopes that one day I
    would discover the light
    within

They never stop praying for
    the day
I would manifest sunshine
This little light of mine
I am going to let it shine
Let it shine
Let it shine.

I'm Sorry

I am sincerely sorry for my
    actions
For my participation in
    dictating the fate of God's
    creation
May mercy be on me, around
    me
May love and grace surround
    me
May I drown in the blood of
    forgiveness
God, Jehovah, Allah as my
    witness
I fast and pray and meditate
    every day
To see the day of grace

As I strive to forgive myself
    and put a smile upon my
    face
But the darkness of my past
    I cannot erase
Life is not a race
There is no winner, there is
    no loser
There is no competition
There is no superstition
Open your heart and your
    mind and be guided by
    your divine intuition
Because the Creator is
    fishing
In every experience in this
    life is a part of His divine
    vision
I am truly grateful, humble,

and thankful
To be delivered from this
    dark prison of 35 years
I hope someone listens.

No One Listens

No one listens
So we never hear
If you care, lend me your
    ear
Believe me, I am challenging
    all my fears to share what
    you're about to hear
But you must listen to
    receive me
Connect with your intuition
    to believe me
Allow the vibration of my
    energy to enter in
Embrace the electricity of
    my individuality

Can you hear me speak a
  very unique language
Can you feel the fulfillment
  of my will
My words are in motion
But I am still
Can you feel my presence
    as I express the beauty of
    His essence
Can you hear the voice from
  within
Quiet your mind and listen
  and you will begin to hear
Believe me, you will hear His
  voice
Your vision will be crystal
  clear
You will remember why you
  came here

You have a great reason to
  be here
So learn to listen to the
  divine voice within
So you can make the right
  choice
I pray you can hear God's
  voice.

The only way out is within

FRONT LINE

Let's Meditate

Let's meditate together
Let's draw from each other's
    energy so we can elevate
In the silence of our mind
Let's demonstrate as one
Let's harness our will
Activate our chakras
They are in motion but we
    are still

Let go of the ego and feel
    the echo
Allow the electricity within
    to resonate
Give permission to my words
    to penetrate

As we, together, dictate
     our own fate
Here and now at this
     moment in time

Let us fashion into shape
Master and create
Out of the darkness of
     our mind
Let us escape
Release the wait
Allow the universal
     frequency to resonate

Can you feel your soul,
     body, and mind
Vibrate in synchronicity at
     the same time
Welcome to the Divine

Let's marinate in this sacred
	place
Free in this sacred space
Free to breathe as we
	embrace
The taste of each breath

In Hell we dwell until we
	exhale
Exit from Hell, leave
Breathe, breathe, breathe
Leave the past behind
As we continue to meditate
As we drift into the abyss
I know you can feel the light
Don't resist
Your first eye is awakening
And soon you will see
Your light body

Your true identity

You are a reflection of me
  and
We are a reflection of Him
And He is pure electricity
She is positive and negative
The oneness of eternal life
Divine balance is your
  birthright
Divine silence, it is your
  choice
Only you possess the will to
  quiet your inner voice

The riot within
The revenge
The regret
The root of your neglect

Your search for self-respect
It is finally time to connect
   with your intellect

You are divine intelligence
A unique expression of the
   Creator's imagination
A masterpiece
A one of a kind
   demonstration
Everything in creation was
   created to serve you
You are worthy
You deserve U
And every gift that is
   coming to you
But you are the greatest gift
   that you can ever receive
The greatest gift that you

can ever give
It's U

I pray that this meditation
    helps guide you through
Your intuition is your divine
    navigational system
Know your destination
And know that your father is
    the Author of Creation
Open your eyes and awaken
And arise from this
    meditation
Namaste.

I Am Alive

I have died a thousand
    deaths
Just to manifest
    unconditional love in the
    flesh

I know where the bodies are
    buried
No cemetery, no obituary,
    no eulogy, no service was
    needed
You see, when you killed my
    spirit, no one could hear
    my scream
Suffering, lost, trapped in
    the darkest dream

You placed my soul on a
  triple beam
My value was a cheap high
  as I digested this lie
You deceived me from the
  very beginning
I believed you
But you never believed in me
Blinding me to see the value
  of me
Causing me to hate me like
  you hate me
You must hate me because I
  hate you

You see, I am a reflection of
  all the pain and suffering
  you've been through
When you see me, you see

    yourself
And it was your self-hate
    that dictated my fate
I know you love the thought
    of me
But thought never
    manifested into reality
You see, you taught me self-
    hate
The knowledge to dictate
    and fashion me into shape
You created a homicidal
    mind
Hostile by design
It was only a matter of time
    before I fell in love with
    my crime

No one knows if you don't

tell, shh
The pathway to Hell where
    the Devil dwells
The road of fear, the selfish
    ego lives here
So be aware when you enter
    into sin
The darkness within begins
    to cover you
Eventually, it will smother
    you

You consumed me, molded
    and groomed me
Prepared my body as a tomb
Mentally doomed
Trapped in the shadows of
    my own decisions
I am not the only soul

burning in this eternal
prison

You see, I know where the
bodies are buried
I am not the only gravesite
I am not the only body
buried in this mental
cemetery
I am not the only sacrificial
lamb
But the day my father killed
me
I realized who I am
I did not die, my soul is alive
Thank you for opening my
third eye, I survived
I forgive you, please forgive
me

This is my resurrection from
my mental cemetery

I have died a thousand
   deaths
Just to learn unconditional
   love in the flesh

I am alive.

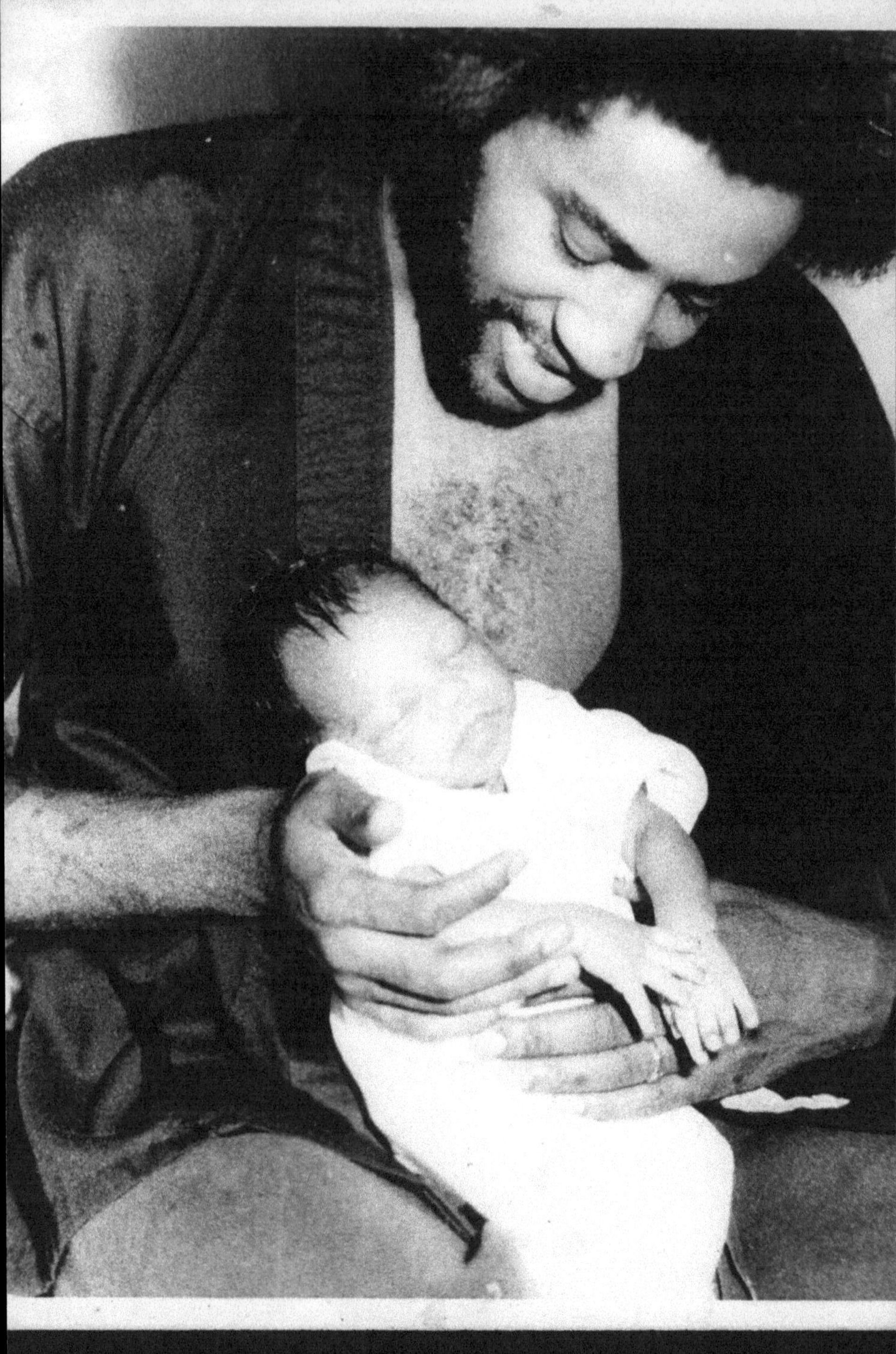

Separate yourself from
negative energy,
don't let someone
else's opinion or
circumstance define
your identity

I cannot imagine how you must feel

I cannot imagine how you
    must feel, fatherless child
Never to witness his face
He vanished like a magic
    trick, leaving no trace
I often wonder how he could
    walk away from your
    beautiful face
Hurting an innocent soul
Forced to grow in this cold
    world alone
Every day wondering if
    daddy is gonna come home

A princess with no king, she

is lost in the midst of a
reality and dream
Searching for love in all the
wrong places
Her innocence taken in the
darkness of infatuation
Leaving her soul forsaken
She's fallen in love with
Satan
A man possessed by his own
pain
Selfishly in love with his own
gain

A good man given a holy
name
But has given into his pain
Hypnotized by the eyes
She has been deceived by a

well-dressed lie wearing a
   disguise
It was too late by the time
   she realized
She was in for a surprise
Nine months later, I arrived

A birthday gift that would
   inspire and uplift her soul
She finally found love, now
   she can grow whole
Five years later, she
   received another gift from
   the Creator
My brother's love would
   elevate her
To a place she can only
   imagine
She embraced the God

within
And her journey to become
a mother has now begun

Once alone, left wounded in
pain
This beautiful little girl has
now become
A young woman named my
angel
Thank you for your sacrifice
Your unconditional love, no
matter the price
Your consistent
commitment, dedication,
inspiration
Your letters of divine
revelation
Your patience

Your passion for life, will to
    fight
You are my Christ

I thank Allah every day for
    your life
Your loyalty to your
    children's life
Fatherless child, alone you
    raised
Two boys to men and we are
    committed to the very end
The breaking of the cycle of
    the fatherless children has
    now begun.

A Mother's Pain

So many mothers and
    daughters suffer from this
In the silence of their pain,
    no one wants to discuss
    this
But the topic of discussion
    is the foundational
    corruption of this world
Abusing God's precious
    little girl
The mistreatment of the
    woman
His second self, the
    co-creator

She was born to make the
    ultimate decision, to

give life
Full of wisdom and grace
An unconditional love that
    could never be replaced
Comfort and guidance
But in the darkness of her
    silence
She has become the victim
    of the worse form of
    abuse and violence
She knows firsthand the
    feeling of being beaten to
    sleep
Drowning in the darkness of
    her bloody sheets
So weak she can barely
    speak

The next day she awakens
    with the power to pray the

pain away
As she powders up her
    cheeks
The make-up leaves no
    trace, at least that's what
    she thinks
Sunglasses cover her black
    eyes as she wears a
    beautiful disguise
But when the sun goes
    down, she is all alone
Face-to-face, living every
    day in a broken home
We all live in a glass house
Please don't throw any
    stones

Fatherless child, I love you
You are never alone.

My determination is beyond
your imagination

Tears of Bondage

This is written on behalf of
the babies in bondage
The children that this world
holds in hostage
Caught in the traffic of sex,
cocaine, and video games
Killing your reflection,
bleeding the blood of blue

As her father continues to
rape her, who would have
known
Her brother knew, but he
was raping her too
Now she's pregnant at the
age of 13

This story isn't told in
    America's dream
Soon as she began to show
Her father beats her, killing
    the baby so no one would
    ever know

The silent cries of our
    children
They grow numb with no
    feelings
Can you hear them
    screaming as they're living
    their nightmares
Fighting their fears out loud
At war with their own
    reflection
Lost with no protection
Addicted to their pain

Dwelling in the shadows of
    their shame

Our little babies are dying in
    vain
It's like they're born in pain
You know the child suicide
    rate has gained
Depression and anxiety are
    on the rise
And after this pandemic, the
    planet will never be the
    same

Now our children are trapped
    in an environment of
    abuse
That they used to be able to
    escape

Now 24 hours a day, 7 days
   a week
They are face-to-face with
   self-hate
Even while they sleep
They are haunted in their
   dreams
These are the tales of
   nightmares
That little kids don't share
Because they believe no one
   really cares

If you follow their tears
They leave a trail that leads
   to Hell
So much pain in so short
   time
He was only nine when he

got shot with a 9
She was only seven when
    her innocence was taken
    to heaven
He was only 13 when he
    became a heroin fein
By the time she was 16, she
    was swinging from a pole
Selling her soul for dollar bill

By the time she was 18,
    she had six kids by six
    different men and no
    dream
By the age of 15, he was
    balancing a triple beam,
    manipulating crack fiens
Blood, Crips, Pareu, Gangster
    Disciple, MS13

Putting in work for your
    team
Your mob, your set, your
    crew, your block
Leaving mothers left
    wounded in a state of
    shock
Because their baby is dead
    with two bullets to the
    head
And one to the heart
Left lost in the dark, where
    does the trail of tears
    start?

Remember Me

Remember me
The me that you never see
The treasure within is my
   true identity
Me, I am chi
I am how you feel
I fulfill my will
When the whole world is in
   motion
I am still

I am the author of thoughts
   spoken out loud
I dwell in the quietness of
   that sacred place
The essence of that sacred

  space
I am here
I am present
I am now
I was not born
So I do not die
I am pure energy
My Father is infinity
I am a child of Eternity
Remember me

I am your destiny
You are so much more
Than your physical body
The flesh that you wear
Is your vehicle here
As you travel through the
    atmosphere
Walking upon the planet

Earth
Remember why your mother
  gave birth
Remember why you came
  here
Remember why you came
  here
Remember why you came
  here

In service to the Universe
As you learn to love your
  physical presence
And embrace your spiritual
  essence
The oneness of soul, body,
  and mind
You are divine
Now is your time

I am here to remind you that
    you are timeless
You exist in a dimension far
    beyond your imagination
Your foundation is the
    Author of Creation
And you are His reflection,
    His likeness

It is your destiny to master
    your electricity
You are pure light
You emerged from the
    darkest night
You are the artist
The perfection of triple
    darkness
Quiet the riot inside your
    mind

And you will find me
Your identity exists deep
    within your memory
Remember me.

Quiet the riot inside
your mind
And you will find me

War

The God in me and the Devil
  in me are at war
They both can't occupy the
  same space at the same
  time
This is a battle for my mind,
  body, and soul
Only one force can have
  total control
I am just along for the ride

The Devil says put your
  pride aside and die
Go ahead and commit suicide
No one really cares
Swallow your fears and wipe

away your tears
You might as well give up
because you can't win

The God within wages war
    on this world of sin
He refuses to give in,
    refuses to blend
Love is the only energy that
    He can comprehend
We won't let the Devil win
We will fight to the very end
Until then, we hurl truth at
    falsehood
Until we knock out the
    brains and destroy the
    chains that confine the
    minds.

It's Okay to Cry

If you follow my trail of
   tears
They will lead you to the
   depths of my soul
Where unconditional love
   possesses total control
The essence of eternal life
   is our birthright
But we must travel on
   this journey through the
   darkest night

There is sunlight in my eyes
   when I cry
I can see liberation smiling
   at me

Through my silent cries
I discovered an echo of hope

A voice that vibrates within
The language of the wind
The breath of life, oxygen
   within
Words that emerge from
   love producing light
Follow your intuition, you
   are right
In the midst of the darkness
   you are the light
Embrace your tears
They will give you sight.

Today when you open your
two eyes
Don't forget to open your
First Eye

I Forgive Me

Let me introduce you to my
 best friend
His name is crack cocaine
When we met, I was only 11
Instantly on contact, his
 energy took me straight
 to heaven
In his presence, I felt the
 power to overcome my
 pain
It's like I escaped, I was no
 longer ashamed
He convinced me that I
 should be confident in this
 relationship
He gave me something no

one else ever gave me—
  value
As long as he was in my life
  I was valuable

I was worthy
I was worth more than my
  pain
He said it was an even
  exchange
My pain exchanged for the
  cocaine game
All the money and fame
The force and power
The total control over
  another man's soul
That's the power you will
  possess
That's the power you will

hold
That power is for sale
The power that will take you
    to Heaven
But leave you in Hell, rock
    bottom

This relationship becomes an
    ownership
Because you can't quit
You can't escape
The darkness of our fate
There's no separation or
    divorce
Until death do us part

I hate this love-hate
    relationship
After 34 years, I gave you

all of ME
And you gave me death
You left me empty, no
   sympathy
That's what I get for falling
   in love with my enemy
You are not to blame
I take full responsibility
I made the decision
Now I will forgive myself
And deliver me from this
   prison

I forgive me.

My Declaration

I accept my identity
I declare my divinity
I submit my will to the
    energy of infinity
    within me

I transcend beyond the sin
Far beyond fear and pain
The blinding emotions
Of shame and regret
Out of the darkness of
    my intellect

I manifest and project
    pure light
Writing my wrongs right

Speaking my healing into
    existence
Persistent, consistent,
    and committed

Galaxies of infinite energy
    exist within me
I can perceive beyond the
    misery of this Earth
The pain of this physical
    birth is worth the
    journey to eternity.

I'm Tired of Thinking

Many people fear this
But this is suicide awareness
The darkest side of your
  mind
Where you feel blind and
  confined
This reality transcends your
  title
Your age, race, gender,
  religion
And even your Holy Bible

You cannot pray depression
  away
The ego wants you to

believe that it is here
to stay
This trauma starts at a
very young age
In some way, shape, or form
We've all fell victim to this
dark cage

Full of rage and regret
When we have lost our will
and our intellect
But most of all our self-
respect
Blinded by the type of noise
that you can't see
Drowning in the endless
tears of poverty
Starving to be free

For only if you could see
For only if you could see
For only if you could see
The pain that dwells
    within me

So we self-medicate
As we demonstrate a
    reflection of our own
    self-hate

We've been conditioned
    to manipulate
Hiding behind the broken
    shadows of our past
Staring into a cracked
    glass
The image that we see
Who we appear to be

Leaves us in a state of
    misery

Haunted by the reflection
We feel lost with no
    protection
Such a hopeless perception
Self-destruction is the
    weapon

You see, I'd rather be taken
    by death
So this is my final breath
I have failed this test
I can no longer live under
    this stress
I am beyond depressed
This is anxiety at its best

I give up
I quit
I confess
I am tired of thinking.

Will you help me heal?

Will you fight for me
Sacrifice, lay down your life
  for me
Are you willing to give and
  forgive
So I can live free
From the insecurity of being
  alone
Will you help me find my
  way back home

Will you save me from
  myself
Is it too late for me to
  escape

The depression of self-hate
Will the pain of my past
Continue to dictate my fate
Fashioning me into shape
Dwelling in the darkness of
   the decisions
I made or did not make

Suffering in silence
Ashamed to speak
Trapped in fear
How could you lead me here
Father, how could you leave
   me here to suffer and die
Why
How can you deny
The lie
The deception
The mental manipulation

I was convinced that my
    father was Satan
So I must be the son of the
    Devil
As my deceptive intelligence
    grew
Lost in the passion of my
    pain
Who would have knew
What I was about to do
Everything we've been
    through
Now I am face-to-face
About to kill you

I've been dying inside daily
So maybe this is my release
Free me from this beast
Free me from this beast

I survived the hellfire now
All I desire is peace

Father, forgive me for my
   past
Will you save me from me
Love me unconditionally
So I can see me
And eventually learn how to
   love me
Is this even a possibility
Can you love this much pain
Can I be free from this much
   shame
Will you help me
Will you help me find me
Will you remind me of my
   divinity
I no longer want to be my

own enemy
I am tired of fighting me
I am tired of killing me
Will you help me heal
Is your love really real?

Poetry

What would I do without you
Where would I be
I would not know me
Lost for eternity
In the darkness of my pain
I doubted you
Forgive me for my neglect
For my disrespect
You deserve so much more
  of me

My honor
My loyalty
You are worthy
Please forgive me
I pray you never leave me

Believe me, I am sincere
In the midst of my affair
I truly care, I am here, I am
    present
I will never second guess
    your essence

I am truly grateful
I am beyond thankful
You are my liberation
This is my demonstration
My dedication to poetry
Where would I be
If you did not find me
Define me, remind me
Of my destiny

Where would I be
I will write into eternity

My birthright to be free
I will write for you
I will write for me
Now I can see
My poetic destiny
Thank you.

Secret Weapon

A conversation with me
The me you can't see
Could it be the neglect
The constant disrespect
That might be the reason
   that we can't connect

We keep bumping heads
They say that people can't
   occupy the same space at
   the same time
That means someone must
   be divided because your
   presence is in my mind
When I am silent, I can hear
   your voice vibrating within

I can't see you but I can feel
    your presence
So often I second guess your
    essence
Your reason for existence
But you're extremely
    consistent
You're always here
You're always there
It's like no matter where I
    go, you're everywhere

I can't escape you
Sometimes I wonder did I
    create you
Or did you create me
Maybe by the end of this
    conversation
I will see the oneness of our

identity
Forgive me for never
   listening to you speak
I took into consideration
   everyone else's revelation
   about me
I always looked outside of
   me for their approval
Will the world accept me
Or will they reject me

I would like to introduce you
   to me
The me that you don't see
I am a reflection of He
And we are a reflection of
   him and her
We are the balance in the
   midst of your silence

We are one

I am your secret weapon
Your divine armor, your
    protection
I am closer to you than your
    jugular vein
I am the possessor of 99
    names
I am the author of speech
    and sounds, so I hear you
I am listening
When no one is around
You are never alone.

Whoever said it was easy,
lied
Whoever said it was too
hard, only tried
Do it

Silence Speaks

Even when no one's home
My essence is present
The me within I, that I
  cannot deny
Now our communication
  begins
This conversation will never
  end
Because it really never
  began

Our dialogue is eternal
Written in the journals of
  your mind
Stored on the hard drive of
  your soul

Pure wealth in your memory
   bank
You are the energy that
   fuels me
The light that electrifies my
   eyes
Possessed by passion and
   power to produce
The greatest surprise
The greatest gift
To spiritually uplift oneself
Because your mental health
   is your wealth

This conversation lays the
   foundation
Of your communication
With the Author of Creation
We are a product of divine

revelation
So silence your mind
So you can prepare to
receive
A demonstration of divine
communication.

Slipping Into Darkness

Can you imagine dwelling in
darkness all day long
Embracing the darkest
nights
Lonely but never alone
With the insight and
foresight to divinely
reproduce light
Eternally taking flight
The power of the
imagination determines
your revelation
Such an inspiring
demonstration
To strive to overcome

temptation and damnation

Sentenced life plus 65 years
This man has been a
    sacrificial lamb
He is the definition of
    willpower
Behind enemy lines, blind
But this is all by divine
    design
You can cage his body but
    you can never enslave
    this man's mind
He is so much more than
    paperwork
He is a masterpiece of art
    crafted in the dark by
    the hands of the Author
    of Life

By His permission we write
We recite, we elevate in
    unity
We give thanks as we fall
    into ranks
His glory is the essence of
    our story
And it is His will that we are
    destined and determined
    to fulfill

So stay strong, my brother,
    it won't be long, my
    brother
Inshallah you will be home
    to see your mother, my
    brother
To embrace her physical
    frame

That day we will praise His
  holy name
We will speak it into
  existence
Every thought will be
  consistent
And our actions will be
  persistent
We are committed to the
  end
You are more than just
  my friend, more than a
  brother
You are more, so much more
Than the labels, titles, and
  names that they gave us
  to enslave us

This is my dedication

My divine demonstration
My art for life revelation
That I offer to creation
With the hope to inspire a
    nation
Because we are the hope for
    the hopeless
And the voice for the
    voiceless
And we choose for the
    choiceless to be free
In spite of the reality that
    you can't see
We have been blessed to
    foresee destiny
In eternity

Can you see?

I was not born to judge you, I was born to love you

I was not born to judge you,
    I was born to love you
And I was born to protect
    me from your selfish
    vanity
Because constant
    manipulation is insanity
Taking me for granted
But, granted, I'm thankful
    for my arrival to the
    planet
I am a gift given that you
    never received
I am the scriptures written

that you never believed
I am the best part of the
darkness of your heart
I am God's work of art
The reconstruction of the
heart work
I am possessed by His
dominion
I am not moved by your
opinion
I am one with the mind of
the Divine
He is the essence of my
spine

Abusing and using me is a
divine crime
And it is time for you to pay
You're guilty of neglecting

me
Guilty of disrespecting me
Guilty of deceiving me
And yes, you are guilty of
    not protecting me
I'm a divine treasure that
    no amount of wealth can
    measure
You robbed me of my
    innocence
Now is time for your
    sentences
You have been found guilty
    in the court of love
Sentence to life with no
    parole
For your crime of neglecting
    my soul
From this day forward you

will remain confined in my
heart
Chained to my mind
The punishment of your
crime
Is that I will love you
unconditionally for
eternity

I was not born to judge you,
I was born to love you
You have been sentenced to
love life
Rehabilitation is your choice
Your freedom dwells within
your voice
Only you possess the key to
truly love me
Because, me, I have been set

free
See I was born in bondage
Just like you, slavery was all
   we knew
But if He can deliver me, He
   can deliver you

I was not born to judge you,
   I was born to love you
And I love you more than
   you hate yourself
Knowledge of Self is the
   key to your mental health,
   your true wealth.

144

I AM

I am pure electricity
The essence of the
   Creator's identity
I am a visitor but
I will be here for eternity
The infinite energy that
   dwells within
My carbon body is who I am
My melanated transportation
My unique expression
I am a reflection of Allah's
   imagination
The foundation of creation is
   my inspiration
I am one with my ancestors
They live within me for

eternity
We are divine frequency
Born to destroy the mystery
Guided by my intuition
My intimate navigational
    system
In the darkness of my
    meditation
I silence my mind so I can
    listen

I am here to remember
I am just a reminder

I AM YOU.

Today I Made a Decision

Today I decided to live
Today I decided to forgive
Today I decided to live life
  free
Today I liberate me

Today I made a decision
I declared war on this
  mental state of prison
For the chains that confined
  me
Will no longer define me
And the darkness of my
  solitude
It will only remind me

That I have been a slave
    asleep

Buried in a shallow grave for
    over 400 years
Forgive me, I've been weak
But today I find the strength
    to speak
The passion and the courage
    to fight for what I seek
As I embrace the patience to
    endure
Purified by the fire in the
    midst of this revolution
I will not retire for I am
    destined to conquer the
    Devil's empire

So today I declare victory

148

because I bear witness
That my god is no longer
    a mystery
For His unconditional love
    dwells within the midst
    of me
For He is who I am and I
    am you.

I am learning to love the
person I use to hate

Bob Marley

This is not the beginning of
    my story nor is it the end
But this chapter is where I
    will begin to welcome you
    to my house of shame
So please take off your
    shoes before you enter
    into my mind

May I offer you some water
    or something to drink
I am here to serve you
    something to think
Food for thought to nourish
    your soul, body, and mind
If you don't mind, please sit

down, relax, and unwind

Tell me what your favorite
    tune is so I can play some
    music
And raise a place full of
    vibration to the room so
    we can be consumed
As the sage burns, as the
    incense, frankincense, and
    myrrh fill the atmosphere
Did you say Bob Marley
Did I hear you clear
Yes, so we put Bob in the air
    in heavy rotation
The expression of divine
    relaxation

Don't worry about a thing

because every little thing
is gonna be alright
You are a Buffalo soldier and
   Jah lives
As Bob brings us to a place
   of grace
Face-to-face, we stand here
   in this holy place

I would just like to say
   thank you for stopping in,
   my friend
Please allow the therapeutic
   healing process to begin
From the darkness of outer
   space, where light leaves
   no trace
It is in that reality we are
   created, fashioned into

shape
As the life germ of light
    begins to rotate
Destined to emerge great
    with the power to dictate,
    unify, and separate
Electrify and elevate
To stimulate light in the
    darkest night
It is the process of
    purification through
    prayer and the deepest
    meditation
As you are the reflection of
    creation, please accept
    your liberation
The knowledge of Self is the
    strongest foundation.

Be a Father

From the bottom of my
   heart, from the depths of
   my soul
I know my words will never
   be the same
But I pray that my sincere
   apology will help ease
   the pain

I cannot change the past
   but from this day forward,
   with your permission
I humbly ask for your
   forgiveness
I am so sorry I let you down
For all those days I promised

And never came around

I am sorry for the heartache
    and pain that I created in
    your life
Please forgive me
There is no excuse for my
    selfish behavior, I will not
    blame a soul
I take total responsibility for
    neglecting the greatest
    responsibility to raise a
    child
The greatest title that any
    man can ever have is to
    be a father
To be bestowed with the
    honor entrusted by the
    Creator

To love, guide, and protect
To teach knowledge of self
  in self-respect
To build your self-esteem
And to help you chase every
  dream

So I pray that it is not too
  late that you and I reunite
  and create a beautiful fate
We, together, possess the
  power to fashion into
  shape a brighter tomorrow
Our unconditional love can
  wash away the sorrow
This will not happen
  overnight
One day at a time but I
  am willing to make the

sacrifice
If you are willing to receive
    and believe that my love
    is sincere
We are halfway there
We must challenge our fears
    and forgive
So we can live free from the
    pain of the past
Forgiveness is the key to
    free you and me
So we can walk into our
    destiny

I love you, my child
I put my pride aside

My shame in my pain
I will no longer claim

I will no longer live another
    day in vain
To my daughters and my
    sons
From the bottom of my
    heart
From the depths of my soul
Please forgive your father
And deliver me from this
    cold

Will you forgive me?

G.O.A.L.S.
(God Over All Life's Successes)

My goals before I transition
into that divine position:
I will strive every day to
quiet my mind and listen
to my spiritual intuition
My internal navigational
system
I will meditate in the dark
until I heal the heart
If I become one with the
divine mind and the
shadow of His reflections
He is closer to me than
my spy

He is the author of time, the
  architect of dark matter
He willed everything
  you see into existence
  with consistence and
  persistence

Pure energy against
  resistance
The natural opposition
Negative energy playing its
  position
A magnetic force pulling you
  off course
But the foundation of
  electricity is your source
As you master your will to
  receive
The power that you will

achieve will be beyond
your imagination
You are the fulfillment of
the revelations
The master's demonstration
of creation
Pure unconditional love
The highest vibration.

Light

Shine your light
Shine your light because it's
  your birthright
Shine your light because
  you illuminate the darkest
  night
You give sight, you give
  hope
Your electricity energizes
  me
You inspire me to be the
  light I was created to be

Now I can see my destiny
Shining like a pure diamond
Reflecting the energy

within me
Civilizing my facility
Redefining our identity
So we can see the value of
   you and me
Who we have the potential
   to be
Vibrating at the highest
   degree
Divine frequency
Pure energy

You are the light of the
   world
Tune in to your intuition
You have been sent to this
   planet
On a holy mission only you
   can fulfill

You possess the power
You possess the will
Learn to quiet your mind and
    be still

Out of the darkness of your
    silence
Your light body will emerge
You will see yourself for the
    first time
The oneness of the Divine
And the unity of infinity
Is our divine identity
So shine your light
It is your birthright.

Me

It has been so hard loving
  me
The me you don't see
The me that hates the
  reflection that I see
Sometimes I just don't want
  to be me.

Know Thy Self

I promise you
What you desire desires you
And you deserve to receive
  yourself
Believe in yourself
Know Thy Self.

Love Yourself

Please don't be ashamed,
   it's OK to cry
The tears help wash away
   the pain
You are so much more than
   what we see, you are
   divine energy
That has the potential to
   vibrate at a frequency
To change your reality, to
   guide you to your destiny

So please don't give up on
   your soul
For unconditional love is the
   force and power you need

to grow whole
And I love you more than
    you hate yourself
So don't quit because in you
    lives the cure for mental
    health

True love is knowledge of
    Self
True wealth dwells within
    your mental health
Please love yourself.

Black Fire

You inspire me
The Black Fire in me
The boiling, burning desire
  in me
To break free out of the
  darkness of my misery
The metal madness that has
  enslaved me
The voices that raised me
The shame that caged me
The regret
The constant disrespect
  of my own intellect

You remind me of me
We are at war with our

identity
The fight is in the sky
The battle lies deep within
   the eyes
I can feel your vibration rise
As I witness your battle
   cries

You inspire my tears
As I wage war on my fears
I just want you to know
   someone really cares
Someone really hears
Your voice echoes beyond
   our atmosphere
Out of the state of triple
   darkness of your mind
Emerges a beautiful light
A perfect desire

You are destined to define
    the Divine
It is your time to shine
Your mind has been purified
Give yourself permission to
    decide to be the guide
The world is in need of your
    light, please don't hide

You are Black Fire.

Mystic Memories

Mystic memories I embrace
The sacred space within my
   imagination
In the quietness of my mind
I enter into a state of divine
   presence
Where the eternal essence
   dwells
Through triple darkness
   emerges His light
Pure energy is His identity
As He electrifies the planet
   Earth
Giving birth to life
The Universe is alive
And we are one with the

cosmos
The Most High is closer to us
than our jugular vein
He gives us permission to
wear His holy names
As we travel through the
third dimension
Learning the conditions of
love's lessons
The lesson that pain
produces
Mastering negative energy
Defining our true identity
In the midst of this world of
violence
Learning to silence the mind
And welcome the Divine
May He enter in
His essence has always been

present
You possess the breath
  of life
Love is your birthright
Learn to fall in love with
  the journey
You are on the path to
  eternity
Let go of everything you
  receive
Every one you cherish
The physical will one day
  perish
But you are alive
You and I will survive
And I will see you on the
  other side
In mystic memories.

Father Farrakhan
(Special Thanks)

Father Farrakhan
I thank you for your final
  call
Your Swan song

It was the vibration of your
  voice that saved me
The knowledge and wisdom
  and understanding you
  gave me
The honor and respect of
  your words that raised me
The perfect example of
  unconditional love that
  made me

You truly amaze me

So on behalf of millions
   of fatherless children
   searching
For words of wisdom to
   help deliver us from this
   mental state of prison
We thank you

I would not be alive if I did
   not learn to listen
Thank you for all the
   lectures and lessons
All praises due to Allah for
   all the blessings

On behalf of all my brothers
   and sisters locked down

behind enemy lines
We are truly grateful for
    your sacrifice on the
    FRONTLINE

Thank you for being a father
    to the fatherless
Hope for the hopeless
And a voice for the
    voiceless
Thank you for choosing for
    the choiceless to be free
Thank you for liberating me

I once was blind but now I
    see
Was deaf now I hear
Was dumb now I speak

Words cannot describe my
  gratitude
I am beyond grateful for
  your Father and his Father
The **SUN** of **MAN** is alive

Your humble son,
Abraham Ali X.

I am Abraham Ali

I come to you on behalf of
Thousands of fathers
And millions of your
  ancestors
With a message of
  unconditional love

We know you are locked
  down
But you are not locked out
To all the young men and
  women locked behind
  enemy lines
There are juvenile detention
  centers all across this
  country

There are prisons and they
    are building them daily
    for you
Especially for you, custom
    designed
To enslave your body and
    your mind

So we beg you to make the
    right choice
Listen to the right voice
    within
Take responsibility for
    your sin
The mistakes they got
    you In

They do not define you
Do not allow this detention

center to blind you
To the greatness that lives
    within
It takes time to discover
    who you are
So you might as well let the
    journey begin

On behalf of your father and
    your mother
We seek forgiveness
We may not deserve it
But you deserve to be free
From the cycle that we did
    not break
That we passed onto you
    and now you are going
    through

If we could rewind time and
   take the pain away
Believe me, we would each
   and every day
I know the pain in the
   darkness that you feel
I only pray for forgiveness
And that one day you will
Find it in the darkness of
   your heart to heal

I promise you that's when
   your eternal life will start
And you will discover the
   light in the midst of
   the dark
Forgive me, I am just
   learning to play my part
I believe no matter the

mistake
It is not too late to change
your fate

So from the depth of my
heart
Please let's allow the
atonement process to
start

Forgiveness is the key to
free you and me
So I want to end this
conversation
By saying that I am sorry
I am so sorry
Please forgive me

I know you hate me

I used to hate me too
But it took me to hate
   myself to fall in love
   with you
I love you more than you
   hate yourself
I discovered the light and it
   is my duty
To guide you through the
   night
Help me help you
Together there is no
   obstacle
That we can't navigate
   through

Fatherless child, I love you.

FRONT LINE
FRONT LINE
REDSKINS
11

Don't be ashamed to tell
  your story
It will inspire someone
Even if that someone
Is just you

Thank you for your
    participation
And may the sacred peace
    of silence
Resonate within
Until we meet again.

FRONT LINE

DON'T

QUIT

It's okay to cry

The text of this book was
set in Open Dyslexic font,
16 point to be more
accessible to our dyslexic
and low vision communities.
More information available
at https://opendyslexic.org

The following photographs
were taken by GoodLuckStef
Productions: pages x, 54, 65,
100, 130, 188, 191

Interior book design by
  Gigi Mascareñas